# FIRST FACTS ABOUT
# WILD ANIMALS

Written by Gina Phillips

Illustrated by F. S. Persico

**kids books** Incorporated

Copyright © 1991 by Kidsbooks Inc.
7004 N. California Ave.
Chicago, IL 60645

The largest animal living on land is the elephant. At birth a baby African elephant weighs 300 pounds and is already three feet tall.

Elephants live in Africa and Asia. A male African elephant can reach a height of twelve feet at the shoulder and weigh about 13,000 pounds. They have huge fan-shaped ears and ivory tusks that sometimes grow to ten feet in length. Asian elephants are not as large and have much smaller ears and tusks. Once widely used as a work animal, the Asian elephant is now an endangered species.

An elephant's trunk contains more than 40,000 muscles. This makes the trunk very strong and flexible. It can pick up a single twig or a whole tree with equal ease and grace. Using this remarkable trunk, an elephant can consume up to 350 pounds of food and 24 gallons of water each day. No wonder elephants spend most of their time looking for food!

Elephants love to bathe in water, roll in mud, and spray themselves with dust. This keeps their sensitive skin free from insects and in good condition.

Humans are the elephant's only real enemy. Hundreds of these magnificent animals are destroyed every year for their valuable ivory tusks.

Emperor penguins live in huge colonies along the coast of Antarctica. The largest of all penguins, they are over a metre tall and weigh 45 kg. The penguin's shiny-looking "skin" is really made up of short, dense feathers that protect it from the cold, wet weather.

Penguins cannot fly. They look awkward as they walk along on land with their side-to-side waddle. However, penguins are great swimmers and divers. They feed on fish and shellfish.

At nesting time the female lays a single egg. Then the male holds the egg on his feet for about nine weeks until the egg hatches.

The furry, gray koala lives only in Australia. Measuring less than three feet in length, it spends almost all of its life among the branches of the eucalyptus tree. Koalas eat only the leaves of this tree. They sleep all day and feed at night.

Koalas can grasp with all four feet. They climb trees in little jumps of four to five inches at a time.

A koala baby is only three-fourths of an inch long at birth and lives in a pouch on its mother's body for six months. Then it crawls out and rides on her back for another six months. Koalas are fully grown in four years.

Giraffes roam the open plains of central Africa in small herds. Reaching a height of 18 feet, they are the tallest animals in the world. A baby giraffe, called a calf, is even big—six feet tall and 150 pounds at birth. Within hours of being born, the calf can run with the herd.

Most of a giraffe's day is spent eating. Its long, 18-inch tongue is used to strip many different kinds of leaves from the branches of trees. Giraffes will drink water daily if it is available. However, these animals can survive without water for long periods by getting liquids from the leaves they eat.

A giraffe's long legs are its best defense against predators. They enable the giraffe to gallop at speeds of more than 30 miles per hour. Using its strong legs and sharp hooves, a giraffe can kill a lion with one kick!

The three-toed sloth uses its strong, curved claws to hang upside down from the branches of trees. It spends most of its peaceful, quiet life this way. In fact, the sloth eats, sleeps, and gives birth upside down!

This relative of the anteater lives in the tropical forests of Central and South America. Tiny plants growing on the sloth's long, thick hair give it a greenish color. These incredibly slow-moving animals are active for only short periods of time each day.

The giant anteater lives on the ground. It walks along on its knuckles. This protects its sharp claws, which are used to rip open termite mounds. Anteaters do not have teeth. Their 24-inch-long sticky tongues are perfect for picking up their favorite food—ants and termites. They eat up to 30,000 of these insects each day!

A single offspring will cling to its mother's back until it is half her size. When the mother is ready to give birth again, the young giant anteater will go off and begin to live its life alone.

Although bears are bulky and appear to be clumsy, they are among the fastest and strongest animals on earth. These distant relatives of wolves and dogs are also the largest of all meat-eating animals.

Bears will eat almost anything—honey, nuts, berries, fish, or meat—in any combination. Bears living in cold climates feed heavily during the summer and early fall and store fat in their bodies. Then in late fall they enter their dens for the winter. During the winter, one to three cubs are born. They are very small and need the rest of the winter to grow before they emerge from the den with their mother in the spring.

Brown bears are found in North America, Europe, and Asia. Some, like the Alaskan or Kodiak bear, are huge. On their hind legs, they stand up to 9 feet tall and can weigh 1,600 pounds. Brown bears have long, thick fur and a hump of fat and muscle around their shoulders. Like all bears, the males are much larger than the females. Brown bears are now endangered because the woods and forests where they live are gradually disappearing.

Polar bears are found along the southern edges of the Arctic ice pack. A three-inch layer of fat helps to keep them warm in the icy water. Polar bears are excellent swimmers and divers. They can swim for more than fifty miles without stopping to rest. This bear's favorite food is young seal, but it will also eat fish or even seaweed. Like most bears, the polar bear's main threat comes from human hunters.

Among the smaller bears is the American black bear, who is usually less than six feet long and weighs under 300 pounds. Black bears live in forests. Using their claws, they can quickly climb a tree.

Lions are the only members of the cat family that live in groups called prides. The pride is made up of as many as thirty individuals, including related females, cubs and young males. One or more large, adult males protect and defend the pride. Males may measure more than three feet at the shoulder and can weigh more than 500 pounds. The females are smaller. Only adult males have manes.

Unlike other big cats, lions usually hunt in groups. Within a pride, females do most of the hunting. Antelope and zebra are their favorite prey, but these powerful creatures can even bring down a large buffalo or giraffe.

Lion cubs are born with spots, which disappear as they grow older. There are usually one to three cubs per litter. The cubs are very helpless at birth. After about three years, the young males begin to grow manes and are ready to leave the pride.

Lions are found mainly on the open plains of Africa. The Asiatic lion once roamed a wide area of the Middle East and India. Today, the endangered Asiatic lion exists only on a small game preserve in India.

The leopard is at home in the tropical forests, open plains, and mountains of Asia and Africa. Hunting alone and at night, leopards like to drop down from trees onto their prey. These 100-pound cats are excellent tree climbers. The secretive leopard often drags its kill up a favorite tree for safekeeping.

Spotted and black leopard cubs can occur in the same litter. Black leopards with black spots are called panthers.

Leopards have been hunted for their beautiful skins almost to the point of extinction. They are now on the endangered species list.

The cheetah is the only cat that cannot pull in its claws. It hunts only by day, chasing down its prey.

Long slender legs and a body with a small, narrow head make the cheetah a perfect running machine. A cheetah can run for short distances at the amazing speed of over 60 miles per hour. This makes it the fastest of all land animals. The beautiful cheetah is now an endangered cat.

One of the mo[st] powerful hunters in t[he] Americas is the jagua[r.] This large-boned, heavil[y] muscled cat has incredib[le] strength. A 300-pound ja[g]uar can kill a full-grow[n] horse and drag it for mo[re] than a mile. The fearle[ss] jaguar likes water and wi[ll] swim and hunt for fish, tu[r]tles, and even crocodiles!

The power and beaut[y] of the jaguar is so great th[at] the ancient people of Sout[h] America made it one [of] their gods.

The cougar, also called a mountain lion or puma, ranges from western North America throughout South America. Although the cougar's main prey is deer, any animal from a mouse to a buf-falo is fair game for this cat.

An excellent climber, the cougar can spring straight up as high as 18 feet, or drop down 60 feet without being injured. In some areas, the cougar's exis-tence has been threatened.

Tigers, the biggest of all cats, live only in Asia. A large male can weigh more than 500 pounds and can grow up to nine feet long. Every tiger has its own special pattern of face markings and stripes.

This huge cat depends mainly upon its very sharp hearing to find prey. Like the other wild cats, tiger cubs learn how to hunt and survive from their mother. When they are about two years old, they leave her and spend most of their lives hunting and living alone.

Humans are slowly taking over more and more of the tiger's habitat. With each passing year, this endangered animal is becoming fewer and fewer in number.

Two small areas of West and Central Africa are the last homes of the shy and peace-loving gorilla. These great apes live in small groups of five to 30 members. The group is led by an adult male called a silverback because of the gray hair on his body. He can reach a height of more than six feet and weigh up to 400 pounds. This gentle giant has an arm span of eight feet and is incredibly strong.

Gorillas feed on a large variety of plants as they browse through the jungle. They do not eat meat. Their massive teeth are necessary to chew the tough, stringy plants that are their main diet. Each night they sleep in a different place after making a nest of twigs and leaves on the ground.

A gorilla baby is extremely tiny at birth—half the size of a human newborn. Gorillas, like humans, shed tears and have distinctive fingerprints. They have the ability to stand upright but rarely do so in the wild.

An adult male will stand and beat his chest in reaction to a threat. Chest beating is also a sign of curiosity.

Because of the rapid destruction of the forests in which gorillas live, these wonderful creatures are now on the endangered species list.

There are five species of rhinoceros alive today. Some have one horn; others have two horns. Most rhinos live in Africa, sharing the open plains with many other animals. A few can still be found in the humid, forested parts of Southeast Asia.

The rhino is an awesome animal. Rhinos can sometimes measure thirteen feet in length and can weigh 5,000 pounds. The two species in Africa, the Black Rhinoceros and the White Rhinoceros, are both gray despite their names.

Rhinos feed at dawn and at dusk on grass, leaves, and twigs. During the day they like to rest and wallow in shallow pools. They have poor eyesight but possess an excellent sense of smell and keen hearing. These tanklike creatures are very aggressive. A rhino can charge at speeds of 30 miles per hour, then wheel and quickly change direction.

Both males and females have horns. So many rhinos have been killed for their highly prized horns that they are in danger of becoming extinct.

Foxes, wolves, wild dogs, and coyotes, along with domestic dogs, are commonly referred to as canines. They all have strong jaws and sharp teeth, a keen sense of smell, good eyesight and hearing, and great endurance. Like cats, canines are hunters and meat eaters.

Wolves travel in packs of up to fifteen members belonging to one or two families. The adults are the size of a large dog, weighing up to 150 pounds. The largest, strongest male is the leader of the pack.

Among themselves, wolves are both aggressive and playful. The dominant male and female mate for life and take very good care of their young. The pack will even slow down its traveling so that the pups can keep up. Wolves can cover 50 to 60 miles a day while hunting for food.

Once common in North America, Europe, and Asia, wolves are now rarely seen except in remote areas. At the present time, the grey wolf is considered to be an endangered animal. Humans are far more dangerous to wolves than wolves are to humans.

Cape hunting dogs are found mainly in southern Africa. They live wherever there are open plains. The dogs hunt in packs of four to 30 animals. They have great endurance and will run after their prey until it is completely exhausted.

There is a dominant male and female in each pack. Adults share the raising of pups. All members of the pack take turns hunting or guarding and caring for the young.

The red fox is found in North America, Europe, and as far east as China and Japan. It has even been introduced to Australia. Foxes prefer to live in bushy, wooded areas. However, these crafty creatures have adapted to living near towns and cities, and even in them.

Foxes hunt alone and at night. They eat mice, frogs, and other small animals. The female fox, called a vixen, finds or digs a burrow. From four to nine cubs are born in the spring. Both parents raise the young.

Like the fox, the coyote has also learned to live near cities. Coyotes are found from Alaska to Central America. They are very common in the central and western United States. Despite being hunted, coyotes have actually increased in number and range. Dogs and coyotes are the only canines that regularly bark. Coyotes also have a distinctive howl. At night they like to gather and "sing" together.

If necessary, the adaptable coyote will eat almost anything, including garbage. An American Indian legend says that the clever coyote will be the last living animal on earth.

Most jackals are found in Africa. Usually one or two jackals are seen at a time. They feed mostly at night on small animals, fruits, insects, eggs, and the leftover kills of other animals.

Jackal pups are born in a burrow dug or found by the female. Both male and female jackals help raise the young. Jackals are noted for making a hair-raising howl that can be heard for long distances.

Pandas are rare animals that live only in the forests of central China. They feed mainly on bamboo leaves and shoots. An extra thumblike pad on each front paw helps them to hold the shoots. Giant pandas grow up to two metres and weigh 135 kg.

Pandas prefer to live alone. The all-white cub is the size of a kitten when it is born.

Giant pandas are very hard to find. Not much is known about them in the wild.